SEARCHING

FOR
My Soul
IN THE
LOST *and*
FOUND

A
PSYCHOLOGIST'S
PERSONAL
JOURNEY

DR. SHIRLEY GILBERT

outskirts
press

Dedication

Table of Contents

Introduction

I am a wounded healer.

I have made numerous trips to the Lost and Found throughout my life. Sometimes I didn't even recognize my pieces, sometimes I wasn't even aware of what I was looking for or what to do with the pieces once I found them.

My journey has not been an easy one. Like you, there were times I felt like giving up, but I didn't. I learned that giving up is never an option.

Today, people are giving up in droves. They are numbing out with drugs, alcohol and suicide at the fastest and most alarming rate known. The current statistics are clear that drug and alcohol abuse and death by suicide have reached an all time high. "Why" has got to be the ultimate question? We're in serious trouble has got to be the ultimate response.

Many of us who grew up in the USA hardly recognize it anymore. Whatever happened to kinder and gentler? Whatever happened to having values that respected others, taking time to get to know our neighbors, spending quality time with our children, enjoying nature and being trustworthy? Whatever happened to not feeling the need to lock our doors at night or our cars? Whatever happened to going out of our way to help someone? Where did all of that go?

I believe the age of technology has greatly influenced the behaviors of the human race. We don't write notes or letters, we text or email. We don't pay attention to the person in front of us, we're too busy looking at our Iphone. We live in a world of depersonalization. No wonder people feel less than.

I know 4 year olds who have an Ipad and junior high students who are fixated on sex and sexting. Bullying has become an art form. Giving up on life has become a real possibility for many, old and young alike. The homicide and suicide rate continues to climb. Today, I read about a fifth grade girl who was murdered in a fight during her class at school..

I am a Clinical Psychologist and I find these facts to be very troubling and not likely to change anytime soon. This is a very intense reality for me. It takes me to the depths of my core to examine the whys behind all of this depression, rage and violence. What has happened to bring our society down to such a level? What is it going to take to change it? Is that even possible? Do we even care anymore?

People seem to be so broken, so lost, in such dark places, as though the pieces of their soul are scattered to the point where they can no longer cope and no longer care about even trying to be a functioning human being.

Greed seems to be the driving force and money has become the holy grail, the standard by which most are judged. People are simply giving up--young and old, rich and poor, educated and not, men and women and, sadly, many young people, including children.

To explore this topic fully will not provide easy answers, i.e., why people give up, why people don't care anymore, why parents kill their children, why mental health workers commit suicide, why so many in the world are turning to dysfunctional detours that eventually lead them to addictions and suicides that are now so prevalent. Clearly, there are no easy answers, no quick fixes, no clear patterns that will unlock the secrets of why people give up, let alone, how we 'fix' it, if we can fix it, or even whether or not people really care if it's fixed or not.

What seems clear to me is that there will never be enough mental health professionals who can show people where to look, even if people were interested in looking. In the end, the choice lies with each individual person. This is a very sober piece of reality when we realize that people all over the world are making choices that affect all of us.

There is no universal panacea that will give us a healthier life on our planet. It is all made up of the millions of us making our daily choices.

In truth, I believe we are dependent on one another to create a healthy world through the individual choices we are each making and by all of the ways in which we impact one another, knowingly and unknowingly.

Perhaps if we truly understood and could get our brain around believing our dependence on one another's choices, we might be far more aware of how we treat each other. Perhaps we might even start to care and begin to create simple daily behaviors of gentleness and kindness that could begin to make for a better world.

Perhaps people could walk down the street or ride the subway without the fear of being sucker punched or kicked in the face. Maybe the elderly and the homeless might feel a little safer. I'm not holding my breath.

People are running out of cope. If we don't start to understand and change the forces that drive people's negative behaviors, then things are only likely to get worse, and, from where I'm sitting, I believe that means we're all in trouble.

Shirley J. Gibert, Ph.D.
Monterey, California,
April, 2019

About the Author

This Personal Addendum was written so that you, the reader will have a full understanding of the perspective of my life experiences--written from the trenches, not from an ivory tower-- like many self-help books are perceived.

I am a very unlikely person to have written this book, or any book.

I am stepping far outside of my comfort zone to make myself this vulnerable in sharing personal information about my own life and my experiences with you.

Nonetheless, it is very important to me that my readers understand that I am writing this book from a very humble space. I have spent my life in the trenches. I write about what I know and have personally experienced. My writing clearly reflects my struggles. It also reflect the differences I perceive between being religious and being Christian. That has been a very important part of my journey.

Perhaps by sharing my own personal struggles, it may encourage you in dealing with yours, no matter what they may be. Perhaps you, too, need to spend a little time in the Lost and Found. You might be surprised at what you might find there.

I was born on a farm in a town of about 200 people, in the Midwest, the youngest of three children.

No one in my family ever attended college. My Mother never graduated high school.

We were somewhat of a poor family and my Mother was forced to support us, as a waitress, when my father was seriously injured in an electrical accident which hospitalized him for many months and put him on permanent disability. I was 7 years old at the time. It changed our family in more negative ways than I care to remember. I never felt more alone.

I remember times when we didn't have enough money for a loaf of bread. We raised chickens in our backyard as a means of feeding the family.

Our diet was mostly beans, spam, baloney and rice.

I remember as a child feeling ashamed of where I lived and the clothes I wore. I remember having to wear my brother's underwear to elementary school and how humiliated I felt, even though no one knew but me.

I never felt as though I fit in or was socially accepted. I grew up largely as a latch-key child since I was usually the only one home. I came home from school to an empty house. I felt very alone, isolated and depressed. I didn't know how to make friends and didn't have any. The children in my neighborhood bullied and made fun of me. I didn't have any social skills and hated my life.

My older half-sister married and left home when I was 12. My older brother was out with his buddies searching for new ways to get into trouble. We were not a happy family. In fact, I don't really believe we ever were a family. We were several people who survived under the same roof. That was pretty much it. My mother's mother and my father's father both died when my parents were young children and so my parents never knew much about raising children.

In junior high school, I became friends with a lovely girl. She was extremely pretty, much prettier than me. She came from a broken home. She lived with her Mother. We used to hang out, go to the movies and sometimes attended church together.

One Saturday morning, my father woke me up and showed me her picture on the front page of the daily newspaper. Her mother had killed herself and put two bullets through Linda's head. They were both dead. Linda was 15 years old. I went to church alone that Sunday.

I lost other friends through tragic circumstances when I was young. I learned to hold life loosely. My coping skills were minimal but I rarely shared my pain with anyone. The people in my world were already trying to cope with their own pain. They didn't need mine.

I enjoyed going to school and always knew that I had a real love for learning. It gave me hope. I took my studies seriously at a young age and felt as though I had finally found something I could do well and feel good about. Learning felt safe, unlike people.

My teachers were profoundly instrumental in helping me build my confidence. This was true during my entire education and I looked forward to going to school. I couldn't say enough positive things about the positive influence of special teachers in my life and the difference I believe they made in influencing my personal choices. I loved the praise I received for a job well done. School became very important to me. My senior year, one of them even proposed to me. That's another story.

I graduated high school with honors and was voted "Most talented" senior female by my peers which meant a great deal to me. My high school choir performed songs that I had written. This was the beginning of a creative talent I discovered I had. It reinforced my belief in myself and my desire to continue learning. I received a piano scholarship from a religious college in California but chose a different path.

When I graduated high school, I found a job and lived at home. I carpeted my parent's home and managed to save enough money to get through one year of college. I took my bike to college and felt very excited to be there although I felt I was way out of my league. Nonetheless, I applied myself and had a good year.

I met and dated a man during my freshman year. He was a senior. After he graduated, we married when I was 20 years old. I had no more money to continue my education but I found a job so that I could support my husband to attend graduate school. In fact, I worked two jobs while he attended college.

Just short of my 22nd birthday, I gave birth to a son. I went back to work after six weeks. I worked hard to support my husband who had a math degree and had decided he wanted to be a psychologist. My job, it seemed, was to make sure that he reached his goal.

During this time, I began to feel very empty and unhappy. I wanted to return to college myself. I felt as though life was passing me by. Eventually, I was allowed to apply for a loan and I had applied so late that others were actually turning them down. I got lucky and was granted a loan to attend college.

Eventually, I was awarded several Fellowships and Assistantships which paid my way through graduate school. This made me so very happy. I began to feel as though I was coming to life again. When I passed my Doctoral oral exams,

I went home to a dark house, raked up all the leaves in the front yard in the dark and rolled in them for a long time. I felt happier than I could ever remember.

I had attended college for 8 years, twelve months every year, including 8 years of summer school. Eventually, I caught up to my husband and we received our Ph.D's at the same time. I went through graduation in a wheelchair from just having had a C-section, with 104 degree fever. But, after all these years, I was determined not to miss this event.

What I thought was the beginning of a fantasy life turned into one of the greatest disappointments of my life when I realized my husband no longer needed me since he had now reached his goal.

After nearly 10 years of marriage and three sons (one adopted at 4 days old), he disclosed to me that he didn't love me, had never loved me, that I was not his choice but rather his parent's choice. I went from the highest high to the lowest low of my life in a very short time. I even spent time in the ICU Cardiac Unit at the hospital with my heart literally out of control. I was physically and emotionally devastated.

I stayed in the marriage 9 more years since my sons were still very young when this devastating disclosure was revealed. At that time, I filed for a legal separation and eventually for a divorce. Our 19 year marriage was over. It was the saddest day of my life.

At age 29 I had 3 college degrees and 3 sons and it was more than I ever dreamed I could accomplish. However, the dream crumbled and I was challenged for many years to pick up those pieces and figure out a way to move on. It never occurred to me that there was a human Lost and Found where I could begin to look for the pieces of my Soul and try to put my life back together or that anyone would help me do it. I felt like Humpty Dumpty, broken into so many pieces, that nothing nor anyone could put them back together again. I was extremely depressed.

Eventually, I reached out and got into therapy for a few years and did some of the hardest work of my life, facing demons I didn't want to face, answering questions which I pretended not to know the answers.

I was very fortunate to be in therapy with such an outstanding therapist. My work with him was the beginning of some much needed changes in me. I was a very difficult patient. I found therapy to be so painful but it felt so good when it quit hurting.

I felt like the mess of the month. If it hadn't been for my sons, I think I might even have just given up. I know what that level of hopelessness feels like. I really wished I was dead.

As I attempted to find my way in the world, I was very vulnerable and became involved with a man who was one of the pastors of my church. It started out as an innocent and supportive relationship. However, boundaries were eventually violated and an intimate relationship began.

There were so many good things about our relationship. We had a wonderful music ministry together and he was a strong positive force in helping me raise my boys. We divorced after 13 years and I still carry the feeling the marriage was a mistake and should never have taken place. We hurt a lot of people. My guilt continues. He remarried and has since passed away. I have remained single.

My life was in the dumpster, I was the mess of the month and looking ahead to any kind of positive future looked like the impossible dream to me. I felt like a complete and miserable failure.

Through years of trial and error, many jobs at many locations, I began to recognize slowly that I was beginning to feel purpose in my life again. I had returned to graduate school once again and earned a second Ph.D. in Clinical Psychology, completed 3,000 hours of internship and passed my national board exams and became a Licensed Clinical Psychologist. This was an exhausting process. It nearly killed me. It happened 20 years after I had completed my first Ph.D.

It was only after I completed this program that I began to have any confidence that I could, in fact, work toward helping others and try to make a difference for good in people's lives. It was the beginning of my trip to the Lost and Found and it was very productive.

I spent several years at different institutions treating abused children who had been removed by the Courts from their homes and put into residential treatment centers. Their stories broke my heart. I learned so much from them.

Eventually, this work took too much of a toll

on me personally and I knew that I needed to make a change in my professional life. After more than 5 years, I resigned my position and began working in prisons, treating violent and mentally ill inmates. As hard as this work was, I found it to be easier than the challenge of working with severely abused children. That was the hardest clinical work I ever did.

After working in several different Level 4 prisons with severely mentally ill and violent inmates, I had a serious accident one day in my office at the prison, due to a defective chair, which ended my career. My life as I knew it was over. Once again, I was faced with the challenge of creating a new life.

After surgery from the accident, it was determined that I could not return to my work. I was given a Disability Retirement and my work as I knew it ended. Not only my work, but my life as I knew it, was over.

After I recovered from surgery, I began to think about a way in which I could continue to use my education and training to try to help others. I began writing books. I committed any profits from them to go toward helping abused animals, one of my greatest passions.

All of my books are self-help books. Most people cannot afford to spend thousands of dollars to invest in personal therapy with a psychologist. There is information in my books for which people have paid a great deal of money.

As my books indicate, each was written at a different period in my life and reflects the issues of importance to me at that time.

<u>What are You Pretending Not to Know?</u>, for example, is about the Columbine High School massacre and my experiences in dealing with it. It was a life-changing experience for me and I never want to be that involved with another similar tragedy. I no longer have enough defenses.

I was granted an invitation from the FBI in Quantico, VA to present my findings from this work as a presentation at their facility. This was, indeed, an unforseen honor. I also made a training tape for police officers. In fact, I gave this presentation to at least a dozen organizations in California, including hostage negotiators as well as at law enforcement State and Regional conferences. My work was valued and this was very gratifying for me. Eventually, I found the topic to be personally depressing and I stopped giving it.

<u>Choose to Win</u> is a book in which I liken life as a metaphor to a game of baseball, each base representing 20 years of life.

This is a book which deals with the challenges of all of the developmental process of aging and, eventually, dying. It delineates the challenges of each stage of life and the burden of carrying baggage from unresolved situations and relationships. It also offers a challenge as to how we choose to come into home plate as the game ends--with a bang or a whimper. There is a discussion regarding people in hospice (who are dying of a terminal illness) and their thoughts on dying. It is designed to create a challenge for ourselves about examining our personal choices and the results they are having on our own lives and on the lives of others.

<u>You Can't Un-ring the Bell</u>; <u>it is What it is</u> is a very candid book about making choices and taking responsibility for them. It offers the challenge for people to not waste their time and energy on refusing to accepts facts of their lives they cannot change. Not even God can change the past. The

challenge is to accept the facts of our lives and find a way to forge a positive path forward.

This is the book which has received the most public attention.

<u>Honor Your Journey</u> is a broad-based candid treatment of accepting our lot in life and making the very best of it that we can. It includes numerous questions after each chapter to help guide the reader to better understand their own personal life process. It encourages journaling and meditation as a way of taking positive personal steps toward making changes and functions as a workbook to help this process.

<u>Would You Rather Be Right Or Well?</u> Is a discussion on the differences between the values we put on being right or being well. The reader is challenged with the forces of wellness rather than rightness. The need to always be right can be a very divisive personal characteristic that can create chasms in relationships. This book offers insights into the ways in which our thoughts influence our actions and our communications.

<u>Looking for My Soul in the Lost and Found</u> was an unanticipated book. It was written in response to the current tragic statistics of drugs,

alcohol and suicide. It is my response to offering hope to others to who have none.

It is also an opportunity to share my story in hopes it could help others. In the sharing of it, I have given special attention to protecting the vulnerability of others, even though I include them in some of my stories. I have left out so much I could have said.

It is my intention to make this my last book. It is my final attempt to get people to take seriously the concept of their personal choices, redemption through searching the Lost and Found and find hope for whatever choices could be in their future.

It was written to encourage people to believe they can find their way out of any crisis, as I have tried to do throughout my own life. If I can fight my way out of my convoluted life, so can you.

I believe there is hope no matter what your circumstances may be. There is a way out. There is hope. There is a Lost and Found and it is a gift for us all.

Finally, I wish to make mention of my thoughts

and feelings about making the choice to enter the field of mental health as a Licensed Clinical Psychologist. It is not for everyone.

I couldn't begin to describe the amount of work, money, stress, time, commitment and exhaustion that went into reaching this goal. It really was the impossible dream for me.

I also couldn't begin to describe the vicarious trauma and post traumatic stress I have experienced as a result of my work in this field.

I do not recall a single word ever spoken by my professors about the personal and emotional trauma that could be a part of this career decision.

When I allow myself to recount experiences from my work in this field, they include many painful memories of serious traumas:

-observing a patient electrocute himself in an effort to end his life;

-observing a 7 year child in a hospital where her Mother was dying of AIDS and trying to explain this to her daughter. When her Mother asked her if she understood, she replied, "I'm just a little girl..." I remember having to tilt my head back to keep the tears from running down my face.

-observing an 8 year old child with Dissociative Disorder actually transition to a different personality right in front of me. I had studied it but had never witnessed it.

-observing the presence of evil in the eyes of a mass murderer;

-having an inmate beg me to end his life;

-having my life threatened by a very mentally ill inmate who was capable of it;

-having to close a file I was reading of a police report describing an inmate's crime.....for fear of vomiting.

-standing outside the cells of several men who had kidnapped, raped and killed small children who were on death row. I remember driving out of the parking lot that day at the prison after work thinking, "I hate everybody."

-trying to find a way to have a clinical session with an inmate who couldn't stop crying;

-meeting and conducting a psychological review on a famous inmate who would never again see the light of day outside the prison, no matter how well he functioned within the prison system.

-watching the body language of the children who had come to visit their inmate father during family visiting hours;

-having to tell an inmate that his pregnant daughter had just been murdered;

-listening to a pedophile describe the details of what it's like to rape a four-year old child;

-reading an account in a file of how an inmate remembered where he buried the heads of his victims in his backyard;

-reading about a child I treated who grew up and is serving a life sentence for strangling a pregnant woman to death;

-serving at a hospital during the Columbine tragedy and having to tell students their best friend had died;

-being on call at an emergency room at a hospital trying to comfort a young Mother whose husband, in his 20's, has just died of a heart attack;

-spending New Year's Eve at a hospital, getting a 15 year old admitted to a psychological unit for cutting on herself;

-telling a teen brother and sister in a residential treatment center that their father has just been arrested again for theft.

-telling a 7 year old child that her Mother had passed away and taking her to the funeral.

-meeting with a teen who had served several years for killing his Mother. As he was being paroled the next day, his final words to me about his crime were: "She shouldn't have raised her voice at me; she knew I was upset." He still didn't 'get it' and took no responsibility for his heinous act. I had to wonder who really believed he was ready for parole and approved it. The report I added to his file read very differently.

I could go on and on but I believe I have made the point that this level of trauma does, indeed, have an effect over a period of years. The word "stress" has taken on new meaning for me.

Also, I am a sensitive Soul. What most people read intellectually, I feel emotionally. I believe this quality made me more effective in my work but took a greater toll on me than my colleagues. Also, my painful early years took their toll on what I brought to the table to take on this challenge. I was already very damaged.

While I would never want to discourage anyone from going into this field of study, I would encourage them to give some serious thought as to the potential personal price tag attached to this choice.

It has only been since I retired that I have realized the full force of the trauma on my life that was so insidious. I refuse to watch movies with violence of any kind to human beings or animals. I cannot tolerate it. I have used up my defenses.

I live a fairly private life. I have a dog I love just a little less than I love my sons (probably a little more than my sons some days:-). I have a weekly massage. I joined a health club and try to get there three days a week to simply walk in the heated therapy pool to help my damaged body.

As I have aged, I am more aware of the damage of my prison accident to my body. I live with chronic pain and am challenged everyday to manage it and work on making healthy choices, no matter what! I have forgotten how a good night's sleep feels.

I am extremely cautious about taking pain medications. Although I have a medicine cabinet that is well stocked, I am immensely cautious about going down that path. My fear is that if I started, I would never get off it. I hope I can maintain this decision and that it does not turn into a detour for me. I have treated many people who were addicted.

Some days, I wish I had stayed barefoot and pregnant. Other days, I feel incredibly blessed to have had the many opportunities, education and professional life that has been so gratifying.

If I'm really honest, however, one thing is certain, at the end of the day I would not honestly wish my life on anyone. However, I am enormously gratified in being confident that it is my faith in God that has empowered and sustained me, as well as provided me the strength to manage the traumas

For whatever reason, this is the life I chose, and I am grateful for it and all the learning challenges it has presented me and created the person I am today.

I will always be grateful for the existence of the Lost and Found in my life. When I got honest about really exploring it, I began to find and make sense of the pieces and how they needed to fit together.

I learned that this honest effort kept hope alive and took me to positive places and people. I learned that knowledge is very different from wisdom and I've learned to see the value, strength and beauty of humility.

CHAPTER ONE

The Lost and Found

The Lost and Found, if we're really honest, is a place where most of us have found ourselves at some point in our lives. In fact, some people seem to have taken up residence there. They spend a lot of their time there, still trying to identify the pieces that belong to them. Further, they often feel clueless as to what to do with them.

They need, and sometimes ask for help, but it is slow in coming, if at all. I spent a lot of time there.

Coming to a point where hope looks bleak and choices seem few, people search for little pieces of their soul that might restore their hope in believing they could have the strength to keep on keeping on and find a way to get off of their dysfunctional path and miserable life. I've been there, more than once.

Maybe someone met us there, joined our

search, and encouraged us by helping us look for those pieces, maybe a best friend or a therapist, or an angel.

This may have felt like our last opportunity for turning our lives around in our efforts to let go of all that was between us and living a lifetime of hopelessness. In fact this is the reason that rehabilitation centers, drug programs and Alcoholic Anonymous were created. It is the basis for furthering the cause and the existence of mental health. Loving, caring friends are some of the best therapists I know. Come to think of it, I don't have any friendships with other psychologists.

As dysfunctional as we sometimes feel on our chosen path, heavy with despair and addictions it often feels like our best friend. It is what we know. It is predictable, crappy and familiar. While we are being led down a path we know is deadly, at least we know where we're going...... looking straight up to see the bottom! The problem is not only the toll our choices are taking on us, but on many others as well.

I've known alcoholics who have stopped drinking but feel as though they have lost their best friend.....the one they could tell anything and not be judged. They can't numb out anymore and some decide it's just not worth the pain.

We usually know we either have to let our dysfunctional choices be in control, or seek change by reaching out to someone for help. At some point we need to ask ourselves the question, "What am I pretending not to know?" Perhaps the answer is that we need to stop what we're doing and find a way to make some changes.

This describes the state of mind and heart that many of my patients had when we began our work together--looking for someone to help them to look for pieces of their soul in the Lost and Found. I went there with several of them because I knew the way. I had created a path there from my frequent visits.

Our painful life experiences sometimes motivate us to turn to drugs, in some form, to alter how we feel, think and behave, especially those which help us numb out and give us some temporary relief from our pain. What may start off as a means of relieving pain often becomes the beginning of an addiction that could even lead to death. Pharmacists across our country complain that they can't keep enough opioids in stock.

Desperate people do desperate things. Many of the inmates I treated remembered starting down the dysfunctional path which eventually resulted in their current residence--a prison cell for the rest of their lives.

Fentanyl appears to be the most current drug of choice, one hundred times more potent than morphine. Police recently have conducted raids and confiscated enough of it to kill many millions of people.

Clearly, greed is the driving force. It is a dysfunctional detour, one of the deadliest! It appears to be a universal goal for many human beings throughout the world. It is right up there with sex trafficking, a 150 billion dollar a year business designed to destroy the hearts and souls of children and young people all over the world. What are we doing?!

While drugs, alcohol, suicide and sex trafficking get most of the attention, there is another horrific dynamic going on which is killing hundreds of our young people. It's called bullying.

Somehow, bullying has almost become an art

form, a recipe for destroying another person by getting them to destroy themselves. Children as young as 9 years old have been reported to end their life because they just couldn't take any more negative abuse or trauma.

Recently, two survivors of the Parkland High School mass shooting killed themselves because of survivor's guilt. And, a father from the Sandy Hook School where his young daughter was killed also took his life. People run out of cope. Sometimes they are the people we would least expect.

They were bright people who had their whole lives ahead of them. What a horrible outcome of someone's choice to terrorize a school and kill so many young students. I believe we will continue to witness the fallout.

As John Powell once said, "Our lives are shaped by those who loved us, and those who refused to love us." We see the evidence and personally experience this truism every day of our lives.

Many years ago, a psychologist by the name of Dr. John Bradshaw referred to this dynamic as "soul murder." That was before we had even heard about bullying. Many children face terrible abuse, not only at home, but also from their peers everyday they are in school as do adults in the workplace. I recently read about a five year old boy who refused to ride the school bus because of bullying. The police found him walking on the highway toward his school. This is a tragic example of what our world has become. What has happened to our human values?

It is little wonder that many children turn to violent behaviors, such as the tragedy at Columbine High School in Colorado. I was part of the team dealing with that process and will never forget the devastating impact it had on so very many people. I remember that a mother of a student who was shot and paralyzed was admitted to the psychiatric ward to help her deal with her daughter's trauma. However, when the mother was released from the hospital, she drove straight to a pawn shop, bought a gun, and took her life right there in the store. Everyone has different responses in coping with stress.

I was working at the front desk at the Littleton Hospital that night and will never forget the overwhelming atmosphere of terror and grief in the crowded waiting area. I also will not forget

33

holding a tall, blonde senior as we wept together over the death of his best friend. Also, I tried to comfort one of the teachers who was hospitalized. With an out of control heart rate, she wasn't even aware of where she was, she was so traumatized. And, I remember riding up the elevator in the hospital and overheard a physician say, "I didn't go into medicine for this." Everyone was struggling.

Most of the victims of that tragedy had never done anything to cause pain to the shooters but, nonetheless, it cost them their lives. This is yet another example of how other people's choices affect all of us.

I will never forget reading a line from the journal of one of the shooters that turned Columbine HIgh School into a living hell. He wrote, "I'm so full of hate and I love it." That didn't happen overnight. How tragic that no one really realized how disturbed and in pain he really was. He might have been helped.

We all need to take a hard look at how we are treating the people around us, and ask ourselves what it is we are pretending not to know. People are fragile, some more than others. Often we can't differentiate them outwardly. This fact is a reality that produces fear in even the best-trained therapists. We don't really know what the breaking point is, when it will happen or what form it will take, but we see it everyday across the world. Many people struggle with impulse control issues and we never really know how their anger will manifest itself.

From my work with abused children, I know that most of us simply can't imagine their pain. I treated children on multiple medications that were found under their beds or under clothes in a dark closet that were screaming. They were so terrified of life. The media reports these tragic stories every day. I am weary of them. I did this work for five of the longest years of my life and felt as though I couldn't have continued it for five more minutes by the time I resigned. I still cannot grasp the intensity of their anger or what it will look like when they are old enough to choose how to direct it. I find that to be a scary thought.

We need to be encouraging one another, not tearing each other down. We are all very aware of our shortcomings. We don't need others to point them out. This is especially true of children who often endure a constant stream of negative messages from their family system as well as their school. No wonder the Lost and Found is so huge. We need to stop traumatizing each other.

I have spent many years working with troubled and abused children. I often think about the way children complete one of the questions on a Child Sentence Completion test. It reads, "No one cares"..........and they would usually always answer......."about me." No wonder these little people seek ways to numb out from their intense pain. Often, they are left to their own dysfunctional choices and never learn about making healthy choices or about self-care.

Even hardcore inmates serving life sentences have disclosed to me their painful memories of things said to them as children. We don't forget those things. It seems to be the positive things we have trouble remembering. Words matter!!!!

I can still remember the two greatest compliments that were ever paid me. I will never forget them nor the now deceased people who shared them with me. In dark moments, I recall them and they make me smile. Have you and I affirmed anyone today, especially those under our own roof? Is there anyone that is going to remember you or I because of our unforgettable affirmation? I hope so.

People are pleasure-seeking beings. We avoid pain and look for ways to enjoy our lives. There is nothing wrong with this. It goes south, however, when our choices for pleasure cross the lines of wisdom and health. We all enjoy immediate gratification when we are in pain (and, for that matter, even when we're not in pain),

It is a different library we each create as we choose how to respond to our personal detour challenges. We are in control of those choices until they become an addiction. Actually, we are still in control when we make the decision to continue it or find a way to stop it.

I have been told that when people get hooked on crack cocaine, they would crawl through sewers and beg for it. This is clearly a deadly detour. What started out as an exciting opportunity to experience a drug that could lead one to euphoria turns out to be so addictive that it can become a death sentence. Beware! Further, people become very aggressive in committing crimes to get money to buy their drugs. Nothing and no one is more important than getting their 'fix.'

I once listened to a psychologist who was lecturing on suicide. He had worked in the field for a very long time and was in charge of visiting the victim's home after the fact. He also had over 700 actual suicide notes he had collected.

What he related was that, without exception, in his opinion, none of the victims were insane. They understood what they were doing. They were full of the guilt it would bring to their loved ones, but their thinking was that whatever death resulted in couldn't possibly be as painful as what they were seeking to avoid. In other words, they were thinking rationally as to their reasons for ending their life. This is counter to what many believe about suicide.

We know that people who talk about committing suicide are, in fact, at the highest risk of actually doing it. And, if people have made a previous suicide attempt, the likelihood of another attempt is very likely. Also, it is important to remember there exists a very fine line between suicide and homicide.

Suicide hotlines have been invented to provide a resource for people who are intensely depressed. If and whether they actually save lives is unknown to me. I have heard that people who have survived jumping off the Golden Gate Bridge and survived have expressed profound regret for having jumped.

Life is such a complex event.

Once I was given the unfortunate task of contacting all of the patients of one of my coworkers who committed suicide. I felt personally very angry with him as I listened to his patients scream and wail over the phone. I felt compassion for his pain but not for his actions.

While I know that knowing isn't doing, clinical psychologists, of all people, are trained to deal with stress and depression. The uncontrolled variable here seems to be the option of simply deciding to give up, regardless of known solutions. Clearly, knowing isn't doing. It was Easter Sunday. My psychologist coworker had checked into a motel and put a bullet through his head. He had a wife and infant baby daughter. I spent the following year functioning as the wife's therapist, working hard to get her through this trauma......very hard work, to be sure, for both of us.

I have spent most of my life trafficking at the seamy end of society. Some days I wonder why I am not an addict or an alcoholic. I certainly would have reason to be. Some days I have to remember that no one forced me to had to go into the field of mental health. On the other hand, no one in my graduate training experience ever shared with me the potential for vicarious trauma and post traumatic stress as a result of choosing this field of study. This phenomenon certainly broadsided me!

One day I ran across a powerful piece, written anonymously, with which I very strongly identify:

I hold the hands of people I never touch. I provide comfort to people I never embrace. I watch people walk into brick walls, the same ones over and over again, and I coax them to turn around try to walk in a different direction. People rarely see me gladly. As a rule, I catch the residue of their despair. I see people who are broken, and people who only think they are broken.

I see people who have had their faces rubbed in their failures. I see weak people wanting anesthesia and strong people who wonder they they have done to make such an enemy of fate. I am often the final pit stop people take before they crawl across the finish line that is marked, "I give up." Some people beg me to help. Some dare me to help. Sometimes they look the same. Some days I'm invigorated by it all and some days I'm numbed by it. Sometimes I just end up hating everyone.

I remember when my shift ended at the end of a 10 hour day at a maximum security prison, I would sometimes drive out of the parking lot thinking exactly that thought: "I hate everyone." The work was taking a toll on me but I felt I couldn't afford to process it at the time, a big mistake on my part.

At the other end of the spectrum, however, I constantly remind myself that it is important to remember that life can be a precious experience where we understand there are highs and lows, hills and valleys, crises and euphoric moments. We can find ways to enjoy our life if we stay focused and positive. My experience tells me this requires strong boundaries and firm determination. It also requires understanding "It is what is is," and accepting it. There are just some things that are totally out of our control. I find it doesn't help me to become fixated on them. We need to use our energies where they can do some good, and let go of the rest.

More focus and attention needs to be given to all of the good things and the good people who do them. We need to change our focus to being much more positive. No wonder people are depressed. We need to learn to control our thoughts in order to control our feelings, including depression.

We can learn to adapt when need be, and reach out for help when it becomes necessary. There are so many resources designed to help people lead healthy and productive lives. We need to CHOOSE that path!! First, we need to believe it exists.

Many of us need to simply learn to do our best and let it be enough. However, we live in a society where we rarely hear very much about self care or acceptance of self. We often hear how we are never good enough, don't measure up to the standard of where and who we 'should' be. We end up feeling never good enough. We aren't thin enough, we aren't smart enough, we aren't pretty enough, we don't make enough money, etc. The litany goes on and on.

Another factor people struggle with is letting go of the past. Some people waste months and years in therapy recounting trauma and events that occurred in their lives. They are so focused on the past that they are unable to focus on the "now" of life which is all any of us really have. So much time gets wasted obsessing about things we can't change. We can only change the way we think about them and how much power we are going to give them to bring pain to our lives.

I do recall a personal experience in which I was working very hard to rid myself of intense feelings of anger. I pictured the person sitting in a chair in front of me and pretended I was talking to him. The words that came out of my mouth were: "I hate you.....I hate you so much, I can't find enough hate to hate you with...." Clearly, I had work to do. I learned that I had to go through my anger before I could get to the other side and work on letting go of it. That was an important lesson for me.

Not even God can change the past. In my book, <u>You Can't Unring the Bell; It Is What It Is</u> people are encouraged to learn the lessons from their past and find a way to move forward. Otherwise we miss the present by focusing on the past and the future. The topic of choice needs to be about the present, i.e., What changes can I make today since today is all I have?

One change I've found helpful is to reframe things as positively as I can. I often tell myself, "It is what it is." I must accept what I cannot change and find a way to move forward.

Some days this just feels like a fairytale.

CHAPTER TWO

Deadly Detours

What are detours? They are the dysfunctional choices we make in response to stress.

They are our violation of our boundaries--when we cross over, making choices to do what we know is the wrong choice. These violations can become addictions and may have the power to end our lives.

How do you and I handle our stress? This is a question that usually tells us a lot about ourselves.

When I was young, I spent so much time alone, I turned to the church in order to feel as though I had a family, someplace to go and feel as though I belonged. There were many positive things about this choice. However, there were many negatives about it also.

I headed down the deadly detour of "rightness." I would rather be right than well. I tried to increase my self esteem by righteously declaring all of the bad things I didn't do. I was sickeningly religious , dogmatic and extremely judgmental. I became one of those people I largely avoid these days. I was a pathetic hypocrite.

Eventually, I learned that the detour of rightness was also some form of numbing out rather than meeting the challenges head-on and dealing with them in a healthy way. What I failed to understand is that what I was doing was as deadly as those taking detours of drugs and alcohol. It took me decades to really understand and find a way to undo this. I am, by no means, church bashing, just sharing my personal response to it at an early age. I think I may have gotten caught up in a cult, unknowingly.

Deadly detours might include alcohol, drugs, sexual acting out, out of control spending, sexual addiction, manipulating others to get one's needs met, denial, cheating, stealing, a life of crime, procrastination, rationalization, overeating, work, abuse of our children, anger/rage and dozens of other dysfunctional behaviors, including religion. They can be anything.

As opioid and alcohol abuse increases to unsurpassed levels, along with the growing increase in suicide levels in the USA, it would appear that depression and anxiety loom large as people seek ways to cope. That humans desire to avoid pain is a feeling shared by all of us but how we choose to deal with the pain (or not) is the real issue.

I read today that the USA has dropped to the slot of #19 ranked as the happiest country in the world, down from #14 jus a few years ago. Clearly, our choices are not making us happier. Our nation has become more violent and more people are simply giving up. I shudder to even think of what we are modelling for future generations.

The most recent statistic I have heard is that 132 people a day are dying from opioid overdoses, a much higher statistic than deaths from automobile fatalities. Some of these deaths occurred by parents overdosing while sitting in their cars with their toddler children in their carseats behind them.

Highly trained mental health professionals cost too much and the people who really need them cannot afford them. The waiting lists for some forms of treatment are year's long in some cases.

Also, seeking treatment for mental illness still carries a stigma for many people, and it is simply not an option for many who need their services. In addition, mental health workers often carry impossible case loads which leaves them exhausted and depressed.

When people do not have the tools they need to cope with dysfunctions in the world, they choose to numb out by seeking detours with drugs and alcohol and other dysfunctional behaviors, which often leads them to simply give up and choose, in some form, to end their life. They can't choose options they can't see.

Many turn to violent behaviors as they seek to survive in a world for which they feel and are largely unprepared. They often resort to anger and rage as their response to events in their attempts to live lives they feel powerless to confront or manage. These people are so full of rage, they will direct it toward anyone or anything, e.g., sucker punches to strangers on the street or kicking the elderly in the face, or raping children, or just about any negative behavior.

No matter what our detour of choice may be, we have the power to change it. We have to focus and cannot slip into an attitude of "What's the use?" Actually, I used to hear this phrase a lot at home when I was growing up, "What's the use?" It didn't help me, it only fed my depression. We need to be aware of our thoughts because they direct our behaviors. Giving up is not an option.

For me, I had to get over my righteousness. I worked so hard to be so good. It wasn't until I hit graduate school in psychology that I really began to unwind my convoluted value system (or perhaps it unwound me!) It took years to unlearn so much of what I thought was so good. I learned humility and mental health. I learned I needed to visit the Lost and Found and start working on putting myself together solidly..... maybe for the first time.

I don't think most of us admit very easily that we need to think and rethink about looking for pieces of our soul in the Lost and Found. I believe we need to see if we can find some small pieces and figure out where we went off track and begin to try to put them back together and work toward being a fully functioning person. This takes energy and courage, both of which are often in short supply.

This is the kind of work that often happens in a therapist's office. Thousands of people are helped everyday through this process. It can work! It does work! It helps many people. I know that from my own experience as both a psychologist and as a patient. It did me a world of good to be the patient and really begin to understand the humbling process of working on becoming a whole person. I was basically clueless, educated but not wise.

As I indicated earlier, our responses to stress is probably one of the deadliest detours. When we don't deal with our stressful issues in healthy ways, we seek detours to help us feel better. No one wants to feel pain. Often, our detours deal with us!

Immediate gratification from our pain kicks in almost automatically. Maybe we start by drinking a little too much, or we start smoking a joint to relax us, or we become a compulsive overeater, or we may become gamblers to the point where we put ourselves in serious debt. Over time, these things can get ahold of us and pretty soon it becomes our choice for dealing with our stresses. We don't even think about it anymore, we just do it automatically. For me, I just went to church and buried it all.

Helping people get off of their detours and back on the main path of their life feels like the impossible dream (sometimes to both the patient and the therapist). It isn't impossible, but requires extreme amounts of work and commitment in order to have balance in our lives. It appears to be the exception more than the rule. How many times have we heard about famous people who are entering rehab for the umteenth time?! At least, they aren't giving up!

I had a recent experience with a stranger. I came face to face with a woman I had never seen before. It was just the two of us. She looked at me, and said, "I just called 911. I immediately asked her how I could help, to which she replied that she was an alcoholic. Clearly, she had been drinking.

She told me she had made arrangements for the the paramedics to meet her at the grocery store across the street in about 20 minutes. It was clear to me that she was drunk and in serious trouble.

She headed out the door in the rain, without a jacket and was gone from sight. Eventually, she was found in an isolated spot, in a fetal position where she could have aspirated or died of hypothermia. An ambulance was finally called and she was taken to the hospital where she received help and eventually went to live in a sober living facility. I later learned that she was employed as a caregiver at a mental health facility. Ouch!

In retrospect, none of the people she had lived with for the past several months had any idea that she was alcoholic. She was a bright, attractive woman who was employed and whom no one suspected. Thankfully, due to positive circumstances, she was able to get the help she needed. This story is, however, the exception. How many people like that do you and I know right now who might be headed for a similar fate? Maybe we are one of them.

What's wrong with the choices people are making and why are they making them? I've heard it said that people do what they know. I think that is probably a correct assessment.

I believe it has something to do with the way we manage, or fail to manage, the detours we all face everyday. Many of us saw very poor parental modeling of the handling of stress. It is clear that there exists much in the daily grind that has the power to depress all of us. However, through a process of "reframing," it is possible to get past it, not take it in, and move forward. We all need to learn coping skills to help get us through the hard times.

We all need to raise our sensitivity level to the choices we are making, where they are taking us and how they are affecting us and the people around us. We need to make a strong commitment to our own personal health and well being. We need to learn new forms of problem-solving and how to apply them.

In other words, we each set up some sort of library of defenses so as to avoid the issues of real-world and personal problems that deserve our attention so that our approach to them doesn't lead to larger problems, e.g., calling 911 in a drunken state to come and save us, or checking into a motel and putting a bullet through our head.

I'm wondering how it is that people who are trained to know and understand the seriousness of their choices are making such poor ones. I believe it's back to the old adage that knowing isn't doing!

Or, perhaps we overestimate how much we really knew in the first place!! I recently was told about a physician who had his medical license revoked because he was writing his own prescriptions for his opiate addiction. I think acquiring power gives us an extra sense of responsibility but also a great opportunity for crossing boundaries. We see it everyday. I'm sickened by the stories of pediatricians who have been convicted of being pedophiles. Teachers, the Church, coaches, doctors, anyone actually who takes on the task of grooming children to do them great sexual damage.

Crossing over our own healthy boundaries always gets us in trouble, at some level, eventually. Yet, we continue to do it, at least until the price tag becomes so high that we are forced to stop through some form of crisis, or until it kills us, or we are found out. This happens every day....to the educated and the uneducated, the poor, the well and wealthy, people living on the streets as well as in high places. It has become a universal syndrome.

How do we change it? Can we change it? Do we want to change it? Are we willing to do what will be required to change it? All good questions! I believe it is up to each person to make the decision to change it. Short of that, it isn't going to happen! I find that to be a very scary thought! I learned a long time ago that I don't have the power to make my patients DO anything. That decision is clearly up to them. I don't think people actually realize how much personal powerful they have to affect the world.

Avoiding deadly detours requires that we know what the healthy choices are. It requires that we focus and have some knowledge of how to manage our stresses in healthy ways. It requires that we care about ourselves and are committed to healthy and balanced living.

The breakdown of families in the past few decades has left many children with poor modelling from their parents about what a healthy life even looks like. Children learn what they live. How can we expect people to make healthy decisions and avoid deadly detours if they can't even recognize them, let alone have a reason to avoid them?

Everyday, everyone faces detours which enables them to function in dysfunctional ways. Most detours look very attractive and often provide a quick fix for immediate gratification. What most of us fail to see is where that path will eventually take us. That includes the path of "helping" others. That path isn't all it appears to be. Caregivers are some of the most depressed people on the planet.

Experience is a very powerful teacher for all of us. As we spend time on these detours and as we face unending stress in our lives, things usually become clearer though not necessarily easier. Nonetheless, we begin to have a better idea of the big picture and of ourselves. At that point, we may begin making different choices or we may be so far down the dysfunctional paths that we have no idea how to find our way back to the healthy path we once travelled. We can always ask for help! Or, we can give up!

One thing is certain, everyone on the planet is making choices about their potential deadly detours everyday and those choices affect all of us.

We are all in this together.

CHAPTER THREE

Knowing Isn't Doing

Many days, I don't do what I know is the healthy choice. I don't have the right attitude, I don't have a spirit of gratitude, and I'm very angry at the state of the world. Getting back on the right path looks like the impossible dream some days. Other days, I don't even seem to care as I know I should. Truly, knowing isn't doing. I have to keep hope alive and not give up on myself or on people. I often find this very difficult to do. Sometimes I run out of energy.....mental, physical and spiritual.

If all of us were making healthy choices, the world would be a very different place. Perhaps making healthy choices is a lifestyle, one that requires discipline and fortitude and, most of all, honesty. Clearly, it is not the easy path. It is the road less traveled.

For reasons that perhaps no one really understands, people often do differently than what they know is the better choice. Why is that?

When we say we really want something, but

we continue to make choices that take us in a different direction, we have to eventually admit that what we say we want is not really what we really want, or we would be choosing it. Maybe we need to ask ourselves the question, "What am I pretending not to know?"

Sometimes we run across people who have created a "divided self." For example, I remember studying about a great theologian whose books I really admired. After his death there were found numerous pornographic pictures between his sermon notes. This man suffered from an addiction which he mixed in with his chosen profession. How was he able to stay sane in his mind and carry out his work without anyone knowing? The point is that he knew that what he knew, at some level, was grossly incompatible with another part of him. How the brain is able to compartmentalize and allow for these behaviors remains much of a mystery. How was he able to continue on both the tracks of theology and sex and find a way to reconcile them in his own mind? What an enormous hellacious challenge this must have been. It reminds me of the recent acknowledgment by the Catholic church of all the priests who have sexually abused children. This is such a sadistic abuse of power.

We've all read dozens of such examples reported by the media nearly everyday, stories of very high ranking people who turn out to be different than the person they represent themselves to be, e.g., the BTK killer. Their chosen detours are deadly for all of us. To me, it just feels like evil.

I have conducted psychological assessments on famous people who will never leave prison because of their crimes. Some of them we would want for our next door neighbor, based on their personable personalities. They have many positive qualities, along with a deadly side.

I once asked an inmate what it felt like to kill someone and he told me, "My hand got so tired."

He had no recollection of ever "knowing" the "right" behaviors. In fact, my work with many lifer inmates revealed that most of them had no idea who their mother was. They had no history of remembering nurturance or training in how to live a good life or be a good person. Yet, society holds these people to the same standard of behavior regarding the laws of the land as everyone else. Yet, even the prison system separates mentally ill inmates from the general population.

Is this the same parallel concept as putting a group of infants in a swimming pool with adults and expect them to know how to swim? I don't have the answers to this dilemma. I am just aware that there is a chasm for some people between what they "know" and what they are able to "do."

Many make the argument that people do what they know. That makes sense. Education can make a difference, but it doesn't always. More and more young people are dropping out of school and turning to a life of crime, gangs, drugs and sex trafficking. It apparently just feels to be an easier path, but in truth is yet another deadly detour, for sure. Many parents are grieving over their children's choices and feel powerless to change them.

If education makes a difference and yet, knowing isn't doing, where does that leave us? I think it leads us exactly to the state of the world as we currently know it. Until people decide to turn their life around and make different choices, it isn't going to change. Until human life means more than greed, it isn't going to change. Until people who care see something and say something, it isn't going to change. Until people recognize the deadliness of the detour with which they are flirting, it isn't going to change. No matter how many programs are put into place, no matter how many trained mental health professionals exist in the world, it isn't going to change.

I believe, in general, psychotherapy to be a process where people are guided to seek answers that often exist within themselves. They often just need someone to show them where to look. They also need for someone to care about their pain. On the other hand, I have treated patients who have come to the conclusion that they really don't want to change. I guess that is worth finding out also.

I read a fascinating piece of research that examined what makes psychotherapy effective. Is it the training of the therapist, which college they attended for their training, their gender, their office decor, etc...? The results of the study indicated that therapy was effective when the patient actually believed the therapist cared about them. This, of course, sets the therapist up for "countertransference" issues but that is another subject altogether. Therapists are taught to stay objective which becomes more of a challenge when emotions are part of the therapeutic process. I have experienced this dilemma with many of the people I treated.

It was a sad day for me when I recognized that I didn't have the power to make people choose positive changes, no matter how rationally I presented them. Choices have to come from them and I can't make it happen. So much for all of my years of education and training! No magic wand here!

I can make suggestions, show people where to look for answers, challenge people, coax people, confront people, etc but, in the end, it is always up to each one of us how we are going to choose to act. This is such an important lesson for all of us to learn. Everyone has limited control.

The most I can control is myself, on a good day.

CHAPTER FOUR

Depression and Anxiety

Depression and anxiety keep millions of people from leading the life they really want, from being the person they really want to be. They are controlled by their fears. I am living proof.

If I had to identify the single most reported problem I faced in my private practice over many years, it would be patients reporting their concerns with depression and anxiety issues. I believe it is almost universal. Everyone has experienced these issues at one time or another.

There is a powerful body of research that suggests that depression and anxiety are controlled by our thoughts. That is why I journal in terms of my thoughts, feelings and behaviors. I can usually see patterns that match up between how I'm thinking with how I'm feeling and behaving.

Sometimes depression is chronic, other times acute. For example, issues of death, illness, divorce, addictions and many other dysfunctions create immediate high levels of anxiety and depression which are often treated with medications and therapy.

Besides each of our personal struggles with anxiety and depression, each of us also faces having to deal with not just our personal fears and issues but with all of the tragedies and violence going on everyday in our world. It affects us. During my growing up years, depression and anxiety became my lifestyle. It was my life. It was all I knew.

Other kinds of depression and anxiety are chronic which means they are ongoing, sometimes for a lifetime. There exist people who fight anxiety each day to the point they cannot even handle leaving their home and going outside. They cannot give a speech in front of a group. They cannot handle being singled out for any reason at any time. They are slaves to what others think of them and stay awake at night worrying about it. They are tormented people who often end their lives. Part of anxiety may include experiencing uncontrolled panic attacks which feel life threatening. These people are in severe emotional pain.

It has been my experience that pain and anxiety are largely managed, not cured. Nonetheless, they can, indeed, be managed and millions of people everyday give evidence of their power to fight through countless obstacles and maintain themselves. They use their strength in healthy ways which yields healthy outcomes. They deserve so much credit for the way they exercise and apply their good strengths. They are examples for all of us. Many of them are helped by using basic psychotropic drugs.

I was made aware of the incredible strength and resilience of human beings who have been through unbelievable experiences when I spent a week at the famous Mayo Clinic. They seem to be able to perform miracles for people who had given up. This incredible place gave me hope for mankind. It also gave me perspective and challenged me to stop whining about things in my life compared to people with real problems.

Anxiety creates emotional pain which makes it difficult to experience happiness and joy which, in turn, exacerbates the depression and increases the anxiety. It is a downward spiral which is very challenging to treat and to overcome. I have heard fear described as "False

Expectations Appearing Real. That is, we are having feelings about something that we fear will come true.

The concept of letting go of anything is a difficult one. Letting go of people, trauma, and the pain it creates is a very difficult process and often requires professional help. A lot has been written about this subject. There is some pain that I believe no amount of therapy will fix. I recently watched the story of the kidnapping of little Madeleine McCann from her bedroom at a posh resort and the heartache her parents have had to live with now for more than a decade. How do they do it? How do all the people manage their trauma? Where does their strength come from? As painful as my life sometimes gets, I am helped by remembering the horrific pain some people are having to cope with. It helps me put mine in perspective.

Without getting into a deep discussion of depression, it is worth noting that there are many different kinds of depression. One primary kind is called endogenous depression and it is genetic. It is a chemical imbalance which needs to be treated with chemicals, e.g. antidepressants.

Other forms of depression might include "situational" which is related to a tragic event that occurs, e.g, death of a loved one, a serious physical diagnosis, divorce, getting fired from a job, etc. Other forms of depression include bipolar illness, clinical depression and several others.

The primary point here is that depression and anxiety are largely treatable, more so than many other forms of emotional disorders.

Also, a valid point can be made that we humans have reasons to be depressed as we examine the state of the world in which we live. In fact, I have given up watching the news on television. I keep up on the internet but quickly skip over emotionally wrenching stories. This is part of how I work to stay focused and not allow depression to be reinforced in my heart, brain and soul. We must guard these precious organs!

In fact, I believe we need to guard our thoughts because they control our feelings and our behaviors. We are never wise to reinforce our fears.

Anxiety is often accompanied by super-sensitive feelings about oneself. We feel anxious about how we are perceived by others.

Therefore, we often avoid social situations or anything that might bring attention to ourselves. We are often hypervigilant and practice a lot of avoidance behaviors. I still remember my 7th grade gym teacher writing on my report card, "Seems self conscious more than average degree." I hated that she noticed this about me. She was right, of course.

People who suffer from anxiety are not usually very self-confident, nor was I. We feel largely inferior to the people around us and often go to great lengths to hide our feelings. We often perceive others as stressors and avoid them as much as possible. We are often perceived as 'loners' and, in fact, that is a correct perception.

We often live a very solitary life. In fact, some forms of anxiety take the shape of agoraphobia in which people are too anxious to even leave their home. They have a fear of open spaces. This is one of the more extreme examples of anxiety. Like most forms of dysfunction, there is a continuum from least to most..

Some people struggle with phobias which are nearly always accompanied by large amount of anxiety, i.e., fear of snakes, fear of public speaking, fear of the dentist office, fear of heights, fear of the dark, and many others. Letting go of fear is a complicated process. In fact, I believe that two of the most difficult processes for humans are bonding and letting go.

Anxiety is not a pleasant feeling even though it is not always necessarily negative. When we find ourselves feeling anxious, I believe we need to try to understand where it is coming from and deal with it in the best way we can. If need be, we can ask for help. Again, when I have these feelings, I often say to myself, "It is what it is." This seems to help me.

Some people express that they see the light at the end of the tunnel, other people express they see the light at the end of the tunnel and believe it is a train coming toward them. Anxiety is in the eye of the beholder. We all need to be cautious that we don't feed our anxieties. The "what ifs...." will always be there. We need to guard against reinforcing those thoughts.

Suffice it to say that unresolved anxiety will likely give way to some form of depression eventually. It is very important to remember that both are very treatable with professional help.

The point can be made that controlling our thoughts can go a long way toward calming our anxiety. I think of the verse, "Be anxious for nothing...."

First, however, we need to raise our awareness level so we are even aware of our thought processes. This is why I find journaling so helpful. It raises my awareness and keeps me focused.

Some days, it even leads me to practice mindfulness and heartfulness.

CHAPTER FIVE

Giving Away My Power

For the first few decades of our life, we are told what to do and not to do, how to be, how to think, how to feel, what to eat, when to sleep, when to get up, how to hold our silverware, how to have manners and a million other things. We have very little personal power. In fact, I was the youngest child in a family of five people and remember feeling that I never had any power. I always had four people telling me what to do and how to be.

For some of us, it isn't until we finally leave home and begin to establish life somewhere else that we come to have and learn how to exercise power. We sometimes see this in college students who are away from their parent's rules and regulations for the first time and they may have a very difficult time figuring out what their own personal lifestyle issues are going to be. They may also have a difficult time sorting out their valucs and figuring out how what they really believe is different from what they were taught to believe by their parents. This is a very complex and difficult process. I am told that about half of the Freshman class flunk out of colleges across the nation nearly every year.

We learn that life has "rules" that require us to follow. We learn there are rules in our family and that there are consequences when we don't obey them. We learn to drive and learn the rules of the road. We learn about the rules of being a citizen in our country. We learn about rules, usually unwritten, in our relationships. We learn quickly that there are consequences when we violate the rules. Some learn these at home as children with well-adjusted parents. Others are not so fortunate and learn many things the hard way.

Life is difficult. Power is everywhere and there can be very harsh penalties for violations. Perhaps road rage is an example of this. We can apply this example at home, at school, on the street, in college, in the workplace, at church and everywhere else. Power is a very universal construct and it is everywhere. The critical issue, however, becomes the formation of our own rules and whether or not we have the convictions to live them.

Also, there are many different kinds of power, e.g. personal, social, sexual, academic, financial, religious, beauty, intellectual and many others. Sometimes we learn that to get along with others we have to follow their rules and so we do. The problem is that we need to recognize what we are doing and remember that we have a separate set of rules that are truly our own and they are not to be compromised easily. Otherwise this can lead to issues of "self-alienation," not a healthy or easy problem with which to deal. Most of us learn to placate the rules of others for the sake of getting along with them and not causing conflict.

Many years ago, I once got marched off of a train behind the iron curtain because I misunderstood the conductor about where I was supposed to exit the train. It was an honest mistake but it really didn't matter to the armed guards with machine guns.

This was a profound learning experience for me. Very clearly, there was a significant issue of power and my power score was zero. It could have cost me my life. It is one of the only times in my life when I experienced pure fear. Surviving that experience was a powerful teacher. I have never forgotten the lesson. I had given up all of my power when I trusted the conductor to instruct me. To this day, I don't know whether I simply misunderstood. Actually, it didn't matter. The consequence was the same. I was where I didn't belong and had no legitimate excuse for my behavior. My passport was taken and I was detained for several hours. I was never so happy to reboard a train headed back to Vienna. That was a full measure of grace.

The point I am wanting to make here is that we can get into trouble very quickly when we give up our power, knowingly or unknowingly. For example, when someone doesn't like something about us and we change that part of ourselves even though it is legitimately who we are, we pay a price, usually without realizing we have just given up a piece of ourselves. This often happens when people are dating and they learn the person whom they really like doesn't like something about them. They change the behavior but not the attitude. Over time, the old behaviors begin to creep back into the relationship, causing problems if not the end of the relationship. It never pays in the long run to behave as though we are someone we are not.

Throughout our life, how many people and how many times have we given up some piece of ourselves because someone didn't like it? We let people control us. We let people tell us who we are, how we think, how we feel, how we should act. They are not accepting us for the person that we are. Ultimately, this can translate into us no longer accepting who we are or even sure of who we are anymore. In my case, it was "the church" that I had allowed to dictate who I was, what I was, how I was supposed to live and that God would love me more because of it. Little did I realize how much work I had to do to unlearn this horrible lie.

This reminds me of remarks I have heard from people who are in hospice, waiting to die. They often express their greatest regret is that they didn't live their own life, they weren't the person they really knew themselves to be. Their time is up!

I remember as an undergraduate in college feeling as though my professors had no interest in MY ideas. The answers my professors wanted were the ones they told me were correct. There was no reinforcement for being able to think outside the box.

One of the greatest compliments I ever received was when one of my sons told me I had taught him to think outside the box. I had no awareness of this. Apparently, I modeled it, the most powerful form of teaching.

I really believe that in order for one's life to 'work,' you have to be and to like yourself. I wrote both my Master's thesis and Doctoral dissertation on the subject of self esteem. It is an extremely complex subject. What I learned is how important it is to develop a personality that you can accept, regardless of the opinion of others.

So many stories I have heard of people who have realized late in life that they have never really been who they are! They relied so heavily on being a people pleaser that they are not even sure anymore who they are. These people have low self esteem, do not lead confident lives and struggle with having a healthy sense of self. Many of them resent the people they listened to as to who and how they should be. They aren't even confident about looking hard at the differences between how they behave and how they really want to behave. They have been giving up their personal power for so long, they don't know how to proceed to even try to get it back.

One of the most disturbing parts of this problem is that we give people way too much power to impact us. I experienced this in a very traumatic way when I was a teenager.

When I was 16, I accepted a date with a young man whom my minister's niece was dying to date. She was furious with me, and possibly vindictive.

Shortly thereafter, a traveling evangelist came to our church as a speaker for our Summer camp which I had always attended. Payback was about to begin.

Long story short, I had never met this evangelist, but on the last night of his meetings, he singled me out afterwards and told me that he had a "strange" burden for me. He had several negative things to say about me and then called me a "phony." I can't even begin to describe the horrific impact this experience had on me. I had never even met this man before. He didn't know me, but he put a knife through my heart and took a piece of my soul with him. I stood there looking at him like a deer looking into the headlights. I was stunned. I was 16 years old.

He left town the next morning. I carried this trauma for the next 16 years. This is an example of the "soul murder" I talked about earlier. People have ended their lives over this level of trauma. I didn't even tell my parents.

Sixteen years later, when I was meeting with the president of a seminary, I saw a flyer on his desk of a man who was heading up a national Christian conference. I recognized him as that same evangelist I had encountered so long ago.

Long story short, I wrote a letter, got on a plane, and flew to another State where he was holding his conference, found him, knocked on his hotel door and, with shaking hands and uncontrollable sobs, handed him my carefully constructed letter which described my experiences with him.

He didn't remember me!!!

After all of the horrific trauma I endured from my encounter with him, he didn't even remember who I was or where I was from. He appeared at least two feet shorter than I remembered him.

As he very slowly began to have a remembrance of our encounter, I watched tears roll down his face as he apologized profusely, although I felt nothing. That night in his speech he made a statement which I took personally. He said, "Thirty three years ago when I started my ministry, I took upon myself a burden that God never intended for me to have. I made myself a judge of other people."

He was the man I was picturing when I uttered, "I hate you so much, I can't find enough hate to hate you with." This was soul murder. It was absolutely devastating to me. It nearly destroyed me. I was young, lacking confidence in everything about myself, without a support system. No wonder I was in the lower 7%ile of self esteem.

Accompanying me and supporting me in this confrontation was a man from a well known Christian organization that my husband had called asking him to go with me and help me with this meeting. I had never met him before. We met the night before the confrontation and went over the details in my letter.

As it turned out, he was a real help to me in confronting this man. However, I was disappointed and shocked to hear him tell my story years later when I found them in his published sermons in which I experienced him as making himself the hero of the story. First of all, I felt it was not his story to tell or at least, not without my permission. I confronted him, he asked for my forgiveness and I forgave him and left his office. It was a very short meeting.

What he failed to include however, in his published account of our meeting, was that he led me back to his hotel room, returned my letter, and told me that he wanted to take care of me for the rest of my life. Long story short, this was the beginning of yet another painful encounter that required confrontation and letting go. I felt as though I had jumped from the frying pan into the fire.

Five years passed and I ran into him one day in a public place. We were both alone.

His first words were, "May I give you a hug?" His last words to me were to thank me for the contribution I made to his life. I looked at him and replied, "Have you ever thought about the contribution you made to my life?" and I walked away. He has since passed away and we never spoke again. I wish I had a clearer understanding of the events of my life.

Both of these encounters are among the most intense and painful of my life. They have, however, provided me with some very powerful lessons.

For example, I will never forget the lesson I learned about the damage we can create through our judgmental lifestyle that does not come from God. This is not the shape of God's love nor the true message of Christianity. It was a big piece I had retrieved from the Lost and Found. It is never my place to throw the first stone and to speak up when I observe others doing it.

Another lesson is that we are all vulnerable, no matter what else we may have going for us in our lives. We are all exposed to people and circumstances that bring out sides of ourselves that we are surprised by and unprepared for. We are all susceptible to attraction and require compassion, from ourselves, and from each other. God isn't finished with any of us yet. We are people in process. I once saw a bumper sticker that said, "Please be patient with me, God isn't finished with me yet." I try to remember and apply this important truth.

As I reflect on my positive spiritual encounters throughout my life, I find myself thinking about the incredibly positive years of attending a church with my pastor, Rev Les Avery at St. James Presbyterian Church in Littleton, Colorado, a man who truly modelled what I believe true Christianity to be. He was honest, he was vulnerable, he was real, he blessed my life in so many ways. He revered the Bible and spoke its truths.

I will never forget the beautiful remembrances I have of him and the positive impact he has made on my life. I learned there are many ways to present to others our understanding of what Christianity is and what it really means. I still remember many of his sermons and how much I learned from them. I will forever cherish his teachings and the ways in which God has used them to give me strength to face my life.

I do not believe that any of us can lead a healthy life without a true sense of self. We have to be who we are! We do what we are! We cannot live our lives to please others who, for whatever reason, refuse to accept us for who we really are. This can be an extremely difficult lesson to learn. This, in fact, is the reason for many divorces and much human alienation between parents and children.

One of the joys of life I personally experience at this stage of my life is the freedom I feel to simply be myself. I don't feel the need to impress anyone with anything about myself. This isn't arrogance, it's humility. In other words, it doesn't really matter what anyone else thinks. It's what I think when I look in the mirror and see my soul.

What I am very challenged by, however, is being true to the self I have chosen. That requires an unending amount of work and accountability. I have developed a high level of sensitivity between my actions and my sense of peace about them. I seek peace and joy everyday in my life. I don't always find it. This doesn't mean I failed, it means that is the shape of being a human being on this planet. This is the shape of reality, and it's okay.

Some days, I do fail and try to learn from the experience so that I don't repeat it. There seem to be so many lessons than can be learned each day. I find it hard to keep up. I'm more eager some days than others to learn them. Sometimes I just want to be left alone.

One thing I know for sure, if someone damages our soul, we need to speak up, no matter how hard it may be. I am neurotic about not damaging others' soul, no matter who they are or what they have done. That is not my call and I am out of line when I do it. I wish I had learned this lesson much earlier in my life. I would have been a better mother.

I am reminded of a long ago lesson I learned from one of my children who let me know that I needed to be called out. One day when it was raining, as I closed the window hard and slammed it on my fingers, I turned around and yelled at my 4 year son as though it was his fault. I will never forget his little tearful voice saying to me, "Mommy, I didn't deserve that!" He was profound in his remark. The next day, I dropped out of graduate school for a semester since it was clear to me that my stress level was spilling over in very hateful and hurtful ways to the people I loved the most. I believe God gives us the children we need to teach us things we don't learn any other way.

I have learned that lessons are everywhere, in everyone and they come from some very un-usual places. I try hard to stay open to learning them.

Some days I feel overwhelmed by them.

CHAPTER SIX

Never Good Enough

No matter how good we may be at something, there is likely someone else who can do it better than we can. There is someone who is smarter, someone who is better looking, has a better body, more education, has more money, has a better job, more popular, a bigger house, a newer car, etc.

It is a very human quality to constantly compare ourselves to others. Society seems to encourage this. This often leads to never good enough feelings which keeps our self-esteem low and our sense of self in emotional pain. The first person that must be convinced that we are, in fact, good enough is ourselves. Since children are not developed enough to form this confidence, they are especially susceptible and vulnerable to bullying.

Many years ago I recall reading a Charlie Brown cartoon in which he is wearing a medical bracelet. His annoying friend, Lucy, will stop at nothing to read it. Finally, Charlie gives in, lets her read it and it reads, "Insecure." I believe this to be the universal bracelet that most of us wear.

When is the last time you and I took note of our positive qualities? When I have used this exercise in the classroom, students can list 5 negative things about themselves in less than a minute but are still sitting there after half an hour trying to come up with five positive qualities.

There exists so much negative feedback these days. We are all judged and criticized for something every day. Perhaps we need to focus on finding people doing things that are right and tell them so. That might go a long way toward helping people feel good enough. Everyone wants and needs positive feedback. We need to cultivate the habit of noticing and saying something about the good things we see in others.

Authors have been addressing this issue for a very long time. Their conclusions were largely that most people feel that "You're OK...I'm not OK."

Also, as one researcher put it, "I am not who I think I am; I am not who you think I am; I am who I think that you think that I am." That is how we learn who we are, by having others tell us the answer as we process it through our own filter. As Julia Roberts said in "Pretty Woman,": "The negative stuff is easier to believe." I believe that to be a very true statement that fits how most of us feel.

The first time I took a self esteem test was before I was about to administer it to subjects for my Master's Thesis. There was, of course, no reason to cheat because I knew I would be scoring it myself. I scored in the lower 7%ile. This did not surprise me. I was carrying very heavy baggage from my childhood and from my very negative experiences with the church.

One of the conclusions I drew from my own data of this self esteem test is that I didn't behave the way I really felt inside. I couldn't.

In other words, I had apparently used my energies to create a chasm between how I really felt about myself and how I behaved. After all, I graduated with highest honors throughout my college experiences, earned two Ph.D. degrees. What I think I really learned is that it would make me much too vulnerable to act the way I really felt, especially if I wanted to survive in the competitive world of graduate school.

I shared with some of the other graduate students who knew me fairly well that I had taken a self-esteem test and asked them what score they thought I achieved. Everyone of them put me in the middle nineties. They could not have been more wrong. What I learned from that experience was how much work I had ahead of me to find a way to increase that score to a healthy one. It has taken me a lifetime to search the lost and found, make changes, and keep on keeping on.

I learned to understand the reasons for my low score but changing it was another story. Increasing self esteem as it is presented and understood in professional journals is depressing. Self concept is very difficult to change once it is formed. Personality theorists pretty well agree that personality is set by the age of five. That's why early childhood training, nurturance and education is so very important. If it doesn't happen there, life will likely be especially challenging. That fits my experience.

Having a never good enough attitude is the reason why people don't take more risks, work on making positive changes or make themselves vulnerable to others. It just creates too much anxiety.. Others are often perceived as potential predators rather than as potential nurturers. And, as one of my friends put it, "Anyone who does anything gets criticized.

Feeling never good enough can turn into a blame game if we let it. As adults, most of us turn either to depression or to anger, or sometimes both. If it is anger we feel, then we begin to identify the others in our life whom we hold responsible for our feelings. This is a mistake and will cost us time and energy if we pursue this path. It is, in fact, a detour. Yet, nearly every week we hear about someone who killed his coworkers because of something that happened to him and he blamed them. The problem isn't with having legitimate anger, the problem is how we manage it.

No matter whom or what is responsible for our feelings, they are ours, we have chosen them and we are the ones who must take responsibility for them. The challenge to change them belongs to us, no one else. These feelings may very well be causing us more pain than the person who inflicted it (as my evangelist example clearly demonstrates).

What I mean by that is that we must do the work to make the changes. It doesn't mean that we don't hold others accountable for their negative behaviors. Many people come to therapy to spew their venom about the people who have ruined their lives. They may have a point and they are certainly entitled to express their anger, rage, resentment and whatever else they feel. However, at the end of the day, the only way they are going to free themselves of all of this negative energy is to start doing the work they need to let it go. They are carrying heavy baggage which effects their physical, emotional and spiritual health. I know this personally.

I am reminded of a recent story in the media in which a husband killed his pregnant wife and two young daughters, one of them begging for her little life as he suffocated her with her favorite blanket. He is now incarcerated for the rest of his life and had to be placed in a prison in a different State than where the deaths took place, for his own safety.

In a recent interview in which he got honest about what really happened, he disclosed that he hears his little daughter's voice every day, begging him for her life: "Please, Daddy......no."

I am hard pressed to think of anything that might provide him relief from the intense pain of these thoughts. I believe it to be worse than a death sentence. He admitted that if he had really been thinking on the day of the murders, they would never have happened. He had made a choice that has cost him, his wife and his three children their lives. He will never have the chance to change that choice.

I believe there is a critical lesson here. There are so many people who would give everything to be able to take back and have a do-over at something they said or did that changed their life forever. It won't happen. That ship has sailed.

We all have to learn the consequences of our behavior and understand that we will live them every day, no matter what. Perhaps the lesson here for all of us is to really think about our choices before we make lethal choices that will change us forever, and which we cannot undo. We can't unring the bell; it is what it is.

I was encouraged to read the story of the father who made his teen daughter walk miles to school as a punishment for bullying another child. This kind of parenting is much needed and seldom seen in this day and age.

Having a positive sense of self will always be a challenge. The surest way to keep it healthy is to make choices that are consistent with being a healthy person living a healthy lifestyle. This challenge will make itself known to us every day of our lives.

We are our choices--7% or 95%.

CHAPTER SEVEN

Losing Pieces of Myself

There are certain natural progressions in life in which we lose pieces of ourselves. For example, we complete certain developmental stages such as infancy, childhood, adolescence, adulthood and senior citizens. With each of those stages come requirements that we fulfill, as parents, as employees, as a marital partner and many other roles required of us. At the appropriate time, we let them go and move on. These are natural losses.

However, those developmental periods move on and we find ourselves in the next section. Perhaps we have lost a lot during that lifetime period due to many complex factors of simply being a human being living out a complicated life. Maybe we had things taken away from us that we don't know how to replace. Maybe we can't find the Lost and Found.

I am aware that two of the biggest pieces of myself I ever deliberately discarded in the

Lost and Found was my religious self and my 19 year marriage It was one of the hardest and best things I ever could have done to support my mental health. I had developed a dogmatic way of thinking and a lifestyle that represented my most deadly detour. Dealing with it was a very traumatic process for me. Doing the right thing is seldom easy.

There exists another profound loss of pieces of ourselves as we lose people and things which we love and cherish-- a mate, a child, a beloved pet, a deadly disease diagnosis, a stellar career coming to an end, etc. They seem to take a piece of us with them and perhaps they leave a piece of it behind. Sometimes they just leave a big, gaping hole.

It seems that as we age, we are compelled to let go of people, abilities, beliefs, habits and so many other things that used to be a major part of our lifestyle. We are left with memories. Some days, this exchange feels far from fair. As pictures from my past have been revealed, I can still remember the response I have heard over the years: "You were so pretty!." Actually, it reminds me of a comment my minister husband made to me one day: "I took your picture off my

desk because you don't look like that anymore."
I was 7 years younger than he was and wondered
when he has looked in the mirror. Nonetheless,
it hurt.

As I face the reality of now being in the Senior
age bracket, I have lost most of my family of ori-
gin as well as many of the people I loved. My life
will never be the same without them. Life is a hard
teacher in making these painful realities sting us
hard as we experience and are forced to accept
them. We are forced to adapt or become bitter. We
are left to cherish the memories, if we can.

We also lose beauty and physical health as
we age. We aren't as pretty, we aren't as able,
we aren't as quick, we aren't as mentally sharp
and we can't remember as quickly, we aren't as
good at many things as we once were. People we
once relied on heavily to help us are no longer
there or no longer able. Strangers seem to treat
us differently.

An additional burden sometimes includes
people we once depended on don't seem to recognize how needy we have become and do not respond to those needs. This is an especially heavy
burden that many seniors carry. I sometimes

feel it myself. Sometimes I wish people didn't see me as being so strong, a perception I created and must take responsibility for.

The whole process of separation is a painful one. I remember feeling tearful as I realized my youngest son was now taller than I was. It was a little thing but it signalled to me how life was moving ahead and what I would need to eventually accept. We lose our children as they become adults. The love may be the the same but the relationship is not. If we're lucky, we can transition from a parent-child role to an adult-adult relationship. This doesn't always happen and represents a profound loss for some.

Divorce and separation represent losing pieces of ourselves. They are painful and probably more so because they were once the source of great joy and happiness. These losses are especially difficult.

Each person, I believe, is very unique in that the specific pieces of ourselves that are no longer what they once were can set into motion the grieving process. I think we can all identify with what this feels like. How we manage it is different for each of us.

However, we can do a re-frame and take stock of all that we still have in our life. We can have an 'attitude of gratitude' for what still is that we cherish and hold dear. We can make a habit of giving to those relationships and keep them alive. We can also keep ourselves alive by not being afraid to praise ourselves when it is appropriate.

I used to think that if I ever won the lottery, I would have immense joy in giving it all away. After decades of trying and not succeeding in winning the lottery, it finally occurred to me that I could do it anyway with the resources I had.

I have, in fact, begun the practice of giving to someone or some cause I believe in every single month. I don't need the lottery to make that happen. These are little things but they add, not take away, from who I see myself to be. Also, I give 100% of any profits on my books toward helping abused animals. This is my way of being true to myself and perhaps my way of putting back missing pieces of myself.

In the end, each of us has to come to terms with who we have presented ourselves to be throughout our life. We have to take responsibility for all of the choices we have made, regardless of the pieces that we lost or were taken from us. This is about human resilience.

We have the choice to work on making our lives better or we can become bitter and depressed and lead a miserable life.

That choice and responsibility rests with us, no matter what.

CHAPTER EIGHT

Care of My Soul

Is there really anything that human beings have to respect and guard more than their own soul? It is the very core of us. If life has taught me anything, it is this. It is my constant challenge.

Some well known celebrities have recently come together to produce a program on the internet for the very purpose of helping people focus and meditate on their soul. They bring to light the three concepts of 1) meditation, 2) Looking at the Lesson and 3) The Challenge to See the bigger picture. They are offering a 21 day opportunity to guide people through this process free of charge.

I am personally delighted to see anyone recognize the need for the care of the soul and provide people a way to honor their soul. I find this to be very proactive and very healthy for us all. I signed up for their class and am very much looking forward to it. I also have a deep respect for their emphasis on meditation which I believe serves a solid foundation for centering oneself each morning before the day begins. I have found it to make a world of difference in my day and in my attitude. I believe it to be a spiritual process which brings me into balance with my soul and my Creator.

I am relatively new to taking up the practice of meditation. I try to combine it with also keeping a journal. It helps me center myself and helps me to create balance in my life. It doesn't take more than 20-30 minutes out of my day and is probably my most productive time. It sets the tone for my day.

Through the process of meditation, prayer and journaling, so many things and people come to mind. It helps me construct how I want to spend that day. It helps to give me a structure, a rhythm if you will, to my day, to my life. It feels good. I believe it to be a way of honoring my soul, a time of sharing my deepest self with my Creator and vice versa.

Care of the soul is an enormously personal concept. I believe it to be different for each person and, therefore, only each person can know what is necessary to nurture and honor it. Regardless, I do know that when I don't nurture and honor it, my life is not all that it could be. I've learned over the years I will never do it perfectly. I need to keep on keeping on and trust the outcome.

Honoring our soul is probably not possible without really caring about ourselves. Why would we take time to nurture anything or anyone that wasn't really important to us at some level? Sometimes I forget this.

Again, we have to care about ourselves in order to have a satisfying life. Self esteem is the bottom brick to maintaining a healthy sense of self as well as building relationships. Otherwise, we go through life looking for people who will make us feel okay about ourselves. This means we look for people we can use to further our own agenda rather than wanting them in our life because we love them. Is it, "I love you because I need you?" or is it "I need you because I love you?"

John Powell has told us to love people and use things, not the other way around. I believe that to be very true, but I think we all get it mixed up sometimes.

In my book, <u>Honoring Your Journey,</u> I talk a lot about what it means to honor our soul. I highly recommend it if you are interested in this topic. It can be found on Amazon (along with <u>Choose to Win</u>, <u>You Can't Un-ring the Bell</u>; <u>it is what it is</u>, <u>What are you Pretending not to know?</u>, and <u>Would you Rather be Right or Well?</u>"

All of my books address personal and inter-personal challenges along with suggestions for meeting those challenges in healthy ways.

I can't think of any human construct that is more important that caring for our soul. That is, in my opinion, the basis for all human behavior and relationships. If your soul is sick, so will be your life, your relationships, and your choices.

If I care about my soul, I have to commit to making healthy choices! I have to focus more on what I can bring to replenish the soul than focus on what I've lost or had taken away from me.

This is a very challenging process. It is personal. It directs our lives.

CHAPTER EIGHT

Cherishing Wisdom

When we are children, we know little of wisdom. When we are adults, we may still know little of wisdom. In fact, what is wisdom? I think we often confuse it with knowledge or education.

Wisdom is the quality of having experience, understanding, insight, perceptiveness, and good judgment (according to Webster).

Apparently wisdom has something to do with those people who have become disciplined to actually DO what they KNOW is right, no matter what. These are people who have developed highly effective habits which keep them focused and centered. These are largely successful people, many of whom serve as role models for the rest of us. Each of us has decided who those people are for us personally. We all have our heroes.

These are people with a strong positive sense of self. They live out with courage the reality of their convictions. Some have given up their lives for their truths. They are not afraid to think outside the box or give differing opinions that are not so popular. They are not guided by others' opinions of them. They can stand alone when it is required. They are self-disciplined--physically, mentally, emotionally, and spiritually. They lead productive, balanced lives and enjoy life. They have a positive perspective of their place in the world. They are not overwhelmed by the problems in the world but rather do what they can, when they can, focusing on how they can make it better. They are wise.

It took me forever to understand that God had not ordained me to hold up the fourth corner of the world, that I needed to just relax and be myself.

Every one of us is different. We were created differently, have different DNA, family systems and countries into which we were born. We each are taught and learn life, values and goals differently in our diverse family systems. We each develop some sense of self along with our perceptions of others in the world. We each set out own goals. We each experience different sources of joy and pain in our lives. We make different choices. We are each unique souls.

Just as everyone has a soul, everyone has a breaking point. Everyone has personal demons to overcome. Everyone has their own story of challenges and painful paths. Everyone has the responsibility for the choices they make about the life they are living. This is how we all got to where we are. We are our choices. And, as a collective body of choosers, this is the country we have created, one choice at a time.

The reality of this issue came to me recently when I had a personal crisis and realized I didn't have the personal or professional strength it required in order to cope effectively. I had used up my personal defenses over the years and was left undefended! What a depressing and scary realization! It was then that I thought about the fact that I was feeling as though I needed to start looking for pieces of my soul in the lost and found....not a space I ever dreamed would ever apply to me. Where had I left it? In my ever-present drive to be a force for helping others, how did I not recognize the insidious process of losing pieces of myself along the way? Whatever the answer, it was clear to me that finding an answer to this question would not be easy, and perhaps not even possible. This was more pain than I had felt in a very long time.

I began to realize that my set of experience as a psychologist had exposed me to a great deal of trauma. Listening to what it's like to rape a child, watching a child dissociate and transition into another personality in front of your eyes, standing on death row and feeling a tidal wave of evil crash over me. These were the pieces of my soul that were wounded and many of them were repressed.

I came to realize that I was not so different from the population of people who have finally stopped trying in life. Why is it that some of us survive and others do not? Once again, I believe the answer is found in our choices. Actually, this defines what we've contributed to the Lost and Found.

What I attribute to be my source of strength to face the decades of my personal pain was my personal belief in my Creator. I am not talking about religion. I'm talking about a deep faith in a loving God who calls the shots and gives us what we need when we need it, whether it's what we asked for or not.

For me, It is seeking to discern and to do the will of God, no matter what. I can still envision the purple sticky notes I wrote which hang in the cells of mass murderers which reads, "I have a plan for you, a plan for good and not for evil, to give you a future and hope."

I feel strongly about the difference between being religious and being spiritual. I used to be religious, a fact I'm not particularly proud of. I was extremely judgmental of others. If I'm really honest, I have to admit that my experience with religious people has profoundly damaged and shaped my life. Those feelings are very hard for me to express and to accept. Nonetheless, they are true of me and my life. Church used to be my life. I no longer attend, although I've never felt closer to God. At the same time, I'm fully aware there exist people who regard me the same way, a fact I am not proud of. I must take responsibility for my history of behaviors…..all of them.

One of the greatest tragedies of my personal life affected me profoundly. I spent decades in a loveless marriage until I finally realized one day I couldn't do it anymore.

During graduate school, we were very poor. Although I had a husband and child to care for as well as a job to go to, I found time to do typing for students in order to earn enough money to pay for my husband's tuition. As the time grew closer, I was excited about it and put it under his plate one night at dinner to surprise him. When I told him to look under his plate, he did and found the money. He looked at me and said, "No more than any wife would have done." I was devastated.

I felt used. For me, this represented a huge chunk of myself that I gave up, I thought, for the right reasons. I've never been able to answer the question, "Which is worse….to do the right thing for the wrong reason or the wrong thing for the right reason?" I still don't know the answer but I do know it was one of the most powerful lessons of my life. What started out as ripples turned into tsunamis. There is no teacher like experience.

I, like most everyone, have made a million mistakes throughout my life. I believe in forgiveness and grace and it is what keeps me going and trying. I feel as though I have had more than my share of personal pain but I also realize I have a choice about how I choose to respond to it. That is, it isn't the traumas we suffer that define us but rather our responses to them. I believe that has made all the difference. Also, the realization that not even God can change the past. All of us must accept that fact and deal with NOW; it's all we've got!

No one put a gun to my head and told me I had to go into the field of mental health. It was very clearly my decision but I was clueless about the personal impact it would have on my life. Nonetheless, I must take responsibility for my decision.

For me, at the end of the day, my life goal is to do my best, simply be myself and try to let it be enough! Maybe this can work for you too. In fact, maybe it could work for all of us.

What does wisdom look like?

1. It means we take responsibility for all of the parts of ourselves and realize that if we want any of them changed, it is up to us to make it happen. We do this by making different choices.

2. It means we know that life is now. It is all any of us have. It means that procrastination is not our friend. We cannot borrow from time what may never actually come to pass.

3. It means that we work on sharpening our tools of reframing, forgiveness and having a mindset that sees the best in others

and offers them support. We develop a discipline which includes the affirmation of others.

4.   It means that we work on having a compassionate and helpful response to the people around us, especially those who live under our own roof. One of the best ways we do this is simply by really listening to them when they talk to us. This is one of the greatest affirmations people can give to one another. It means knowing what love looks like.

5.   It means that we work on having a balanced life, one that we really choose and is what we want our lives to be. We work on being the best person we can hope to be. We are always a work in progress.

6.   It means we understand the critical element of making personal choices and never intentionally create a detour that will end up hurting ourselves or others.

7.   It means knowing that numbing out is a defense that is not our friend, no matter how good it may make us feel at the time. We also understand that immediate

gratification feels good but is not the best solution to our problems.

8. It means having the motivation and ability to really listen and hear others without imposing unjustified judgment. It means having respect for others no matter how much their opinion may differ from ours.

9. It means we practice loving people and using things and don't get this mixed up with loving things and using people.

10. It means that we cherish, honor and respect our special relationships and do not cross lines that will eventually destroy them. We nourish and cherish them. We take time for them. We honor them.

11. It means that we understand that every human being has their own version of reality and that it is normal for people to not agree. It does not denote who is good or bad, just different. Society has many different versions of reality.

12. It means that we are open to the idea that we may not, in fact, have all of the

answers and need to maintain a love for learning and seek to think outside the box. It means knowing how much we still don't know, and may never know.

13. It means we have a sense of gratefulness for everything and every person in our life for which we are thankful. We never take them for granted.

14. It means that we understand that the hand that rocks the cradle rules the world, that our children are among are greatest investments and offer our greatest opportunity to leave a great inheritance to the world long after we cease to exist.

15. It means that we understand that we can choose to have faith in a loving God who has a positive plan for our lives and exists to help us find our way.

16. It means that we have a realistic view of who we are, what are capabilities are. We also understand that others exist who have greater capabilities than us and we can cheer them on. Their strengths do not lessen our value.

17. It means that, when all is said and done, that we lived the best life we could and can let it be enough when our time in life comes to an end. We don't compare ourselves to others. We simply focus on being the best we know how to be.

18. We can understand that the constructs we hold in our head are the most important of all in affecting the choices we make which is what determines the life we experience. We are our choices.

19. We can cherish the Soul within us and seek to constantly nourish and strengthen it. It will reflect the care it receives from us and be obvious to the people around us.

20. We can face the fact that if do not like our life or things about ourselves, they will only change if we have courage to begin making different choices. Short of this, the world will not change. Change must begin with me or it will not happen.

Wisdom is precious and priceless, and not easily attained.

CHAPTER NINE

My Little Red Wagon

As ridiculous as it may sound, one day while I was heavily invested in treating mentally disturbed adolescent girls in an institution 100 miles in the middle of nowhere, I was sitting at my kitchen table on a Saturday morning and began to make a sketch on an envelope. I was feeling very alone.

The sketch showed me as a small child, holding onto the leash of my dog in one hand and the other small hand in the hand of Jesus. He had his back to me as we were all climbing a hill. In His other hand was the handle of a small red wagon he was pulling. In the wagon was stacked very high all of my sadness, trauma, fears, regrets and anxieties, my soul. Only He was strong enough to pull that wagon. Perhaps it represented my personal Lost and Found.

I began to understand that people, including myself, don't necessarily make right or wrong decisions, we simply make decisions, then make them right or wrong depending on how we manage them.

My job was to learn to put all of my problems in the wagon and follow where I was being led. His job was to manage everything in the wagon.

I was lovingly supported on both sides of me and felt empowered to simply put one foot in front of the other and trust the ground to be there. I love that imagery.

Many years later I met an artist and commissioned her to paint this picture for me. I love it. I believe when I am able to live it, my life works.

At the beginning of my book, it is noted that I dedicated it to my dear and precious friend, Judy.

Judy died on a very cold winter's night in our home as we laid on our backs in a bed next to one another with our hands firmly interlocked together.

She was 45 years old, dying from multiple myeloma, similar to bone cancer, She had been suffering for many years, enduring chemotherapy, radiation and multiple surgeries.

I was honored to host her in our home for the last year of her life and she presented me with a very unusual education and gift of what it's like to endure a terminal illness. I honestly don't ever remember her complaining, not even once.

We spent hours processing her life and her upcoming death. I told her she didn't need to be strong for me, with tears in my eyes. She kissed my hand and said she was sorry this was so hard for me. I will never forget her words, "I just have to put one foot in front of the other and trust the ground will be there." Such wisdom!

On that fateful night, her Mother called me, two stories up in our large home and asked me to come down, at Judy's request. When I entered the room, I could hear the death rattle. I put on her favorite music, administered a pain patch to her body, called her doctor and laid down beside her. She didn't speak a word but the last thing she did was squeeze my hand. My last words to her, "It's O.K. to go….." and she died. I closed her eyes and called her children…

Three days prior to that she and I had grocery shopped. She had pushed her own cart through the snow in the grocery store parking lot. Later that evening, she had a pedicure and we ate hot-fudge sundaes.

I told her I was studying for my Psychology board exams and wasn't sure I could ever pass them. She looked at me and said, "So, what are you, a dumb shit?" We both laughed so hard.

She was the little sister I never had, one of the most precious gifts ever given me. I cherish the life and memory of her every day. She passed on February 2, 1994, one month earlier than my father's passing.

Although Judy wasn't the one who planted the idea in my mind about the little red wagon, she lived it and I think I learned it from her. Such a powerful lesson it was.

Perhaps you can relate to the little red wagon story and even envision how it might help you in your life to not have to carry such a heavy load, or feel alone in the midst of your personal pain. Sometimes it helps just to know someone is sharing the burden and helping us carry the pain.

Each of us can identify those special people in our lives that made all the difference for us. Many of us can count them on one hand. Judy is definitely one of those people for me, along with my precious Mother and my children.

Everyday each of us has the opportunity to make a real difference in someone's life. What we do with it defines us and is what will likely be one of our final thoughts when it is our turn to let go of this life forever.

All we have in now. Let's make it count.

Start with your little red wagon!

Finally, I ask you,

"What are you pretending not to know?

Which choices in your life do you need to change?

How do you want your epitaph to read?

How do you want your children to remember you?

Is there someone in your life right now that you could help sort through the Lost and Found of their life and make a positive difference for them?

What does wisdom look like to you? Are you practicing it?

You and I are running out of time. In a world that is losing its battle for health and happiness, what can we start doing today that might make a difference?

We'll never know unless we try.

Let's do this!

Let me hear from you:-)

sjg11643@yahoo.com

Conclusions

Life is difficult. Otherwise, there would be no Lost and Found, where maybe more is lost than found...where we are constantly seeking to reconcile our journey with our soul.

Everyone has their own version of reality and we are wise to understand this truth about human beings.

We need to use our good energy to find our own way. We cannot give out of an empty cup.

Every human being on the planet is trying to find their way in a complex world. People will never agree about the right or wrong path they should travel. Everyone has their own version of reality.

The deadly detours are destroying lives and creating violence and death in our world.

Evil is not a figment of our imagination. I have seen it up close and personal. I believe it touches all of us in one form or another Seeking balance in our lives is very important in order to function in healthy ways. Self-care is critical to healthy living. We need to get honest about our lives, our feelings, our attitudes, our relationships and especially, our choices.

Maybe it's time to entertain the question of what it is we are pretending not to know and make some changes. Let's examine our personal choices and get real about where they are really taking us. If we don't choose to change any of them, then we can count on the world continuing to decompensate.

The only person who can care for, change, honor and nurture your Soul is you.

Collect the pieces you lost, let go of the ones you no longer need and cherish the ones you still have.

CPSIA information can be obtained
at www.ICGtesting.com
Printed in the USA
BVHW082241270519
549348BV00018B/1348/P